Would You Believe...

bed testers get paid to sleep?

and other jammy jobs

Richard Platt

OXFORD

UNIVERSITY PRESS

Contents

OXFORD
UNIVERSITY PRESS

Great Clarendon Street, Oxford OX2 6DP

Oxford University Press is a department of the University of Oxford. It furthers the University's objective of excellence in research, scholarship, and education by publishing worldwide in

Oxford   New York

Auckland   Cape Town   Dar es Salaam Hong Kong   Karachi   Kuala Lumpur   Madrid Melbourne   Mexico City   Nairobi   New Delhi Shanghai   Taipei   Toronto

With offices in

Argentina   Austria   Brazil   Chile Czech Republic   France   Greece   Guatemala Hungary   Italy   Japan   Poland   Portugal Singapore   South Korea   Switzerland   Thailand Turkey   Ukraine   Vietnam

Oxford is a registered trade mark of Oxford University Press in the UK and in certain other countries

Text copyright © Oxford University Press 2010

The moral rights of the author have been asserted

Database right Oxford University Press (maker)

First published 2010

British Library Cataloguing in Publication Data

Data available

ISBN 978-0-19-911986-8

1 3 5 7 9 10 8 6 4 2

Originated by Oxford University Press

Created by BOOKWORK Ltd

Printed in China

WARNING: The practices in this book are for information only and should not be tried at home!

Introduction

WORK IS AS OLD AS HUMAN LIFE itself. Without it, the world's first people could not have lived. To eat, they had to hunt and gather seeds, fruits and roots. Compared to factory or office jobs, this sounds easy, and it was. Hunter-gatherers laboured for less than half of today's nine-to-five routine.

Work soon changed into something men and women did for a master, in exchange for land, food, goods and later money. By the time these two 19th-century fisher-folk had paid jobs in boats and markets, "work" meant pretty much what it means today.

So why should work interest you? Because you'll have to do it for 40 years! This isn't as bad as it sounds. Many people find jobs they love. This book might help you do the same. It explores the world of work from the earliest times to the present – and beyond.

Would You Believe . . . ?

Who, when, where and how?
Who suggested that workers should govern our world? When did deadly disease double workers' wages? Where would you look for a robot in your house? How do you get paid for eating chocolate? If you want the answers, turn the page.

What is Work?

I T SEEMS A SIMPLE QUESTION, but answering it isn't easy. Is work what you do to earn money? Not always: voluntary workers do it for nothing. Is it the opposite of play? Not really: some of us make our best friends at work. Is it dull drudgery? Not that either: I love my job.

It's true that for all of us, work can sometimes be hard, dull, boring or exhausting. But find the right job, and work becomes the very centre of life: something you look forward to doing every morning when you wake up.

● **What do you do at work?** ▲
A job involves much more than just working. For most of us, work shapes and organizes our lives. The first thing people mention when they're asked who they are is often their occupation. And some people long for the office routine even when they are on holiday.

Would You Believe . . . ?

Painful work!
The word "work" didn't start as meaning a paid task. It comes from the Viking word "*virkja*", meaning to feel pain. Even now, "work" means more than just labour. A good dictionary lists no fewer than 33 old and new meanings for the word.

◄ **Unpublished writer**
Are poets working if none of their rhymes are ever published? They would say, "Of course!" For an artist, the point of work is not the pay, it's art itself. However, without a publisher or at least a wealthy patron (sponsor), artists scratch a living, as the 19th-century German artist Carl Spitzweg showed in this painting *The Poor Poet*.

Work holds intriguing surprises. Some of the jobs that everyone wants, like being a celebrity, turn out to have hidden drawbacks. And even low-paid work is immensely satisfying when you can see the difference and improvement you make in other people's lives.

Former US president Reagan said, "Hard work never killed anybody, but why take the chance?"

● ● ● ● ● ● ● ● ● ● ● ● ● ● ●

Who needs a job?

You may hear people say they'd stop work tomorrow if they could. But half of all lottery jackpot winners keep their jobs, or return to them. Though these millionaires don't need to work, they miss their workplace friendships and the reward of doing something useful each day.

Celebrities in focus ▼

What exactly do celebrities do for a living? Celebs may appear to have a dream job, but in reality, this can be a full-time nightmare. For their high pay, the famous give up all privacy and may have to put up with 20 photographers camping outside their front door. And fame is fickle – a celebrity today may be forgotten tomorrow.

Volunteer work ▲
There isn't enough money to pay for all the work that needs doing. Volunteers plug the gap by working for nothing. This worker provides friendship and help for an old man.

Field and Workshop

Field work ▲
The farmer's work became much easier with the invention of the plough. Hitched to a pair of oxen (cattle), ploughs allowed farmers to turn over the soil in their fields far quicker than they could with hoes.

SPATTERED WITH MUD AND WEARY from the fields, the world's workers were all farmers until around 6,000 years ago. But then, as people began to live in bigger groups in towns, a few gave up the back-breaking labour of farming. Instead they worked at special tasks they could do better or faster than other people.

• •

Improved farming methods made this change possible. The invention of the plough in Mesopotamia (now Iraq) in about 6000 BCE meant fewer people were needed to grow enough grain for everyone.

Babylon bricks ▲
Some 2,600 years ago, craftsmen from Babylon (once a city in Mesopotamia) made these lions for the city's Ishtar Gate. Made of mud bricks, they have survived because the bricks were fired (made red-hot) to make them waterproof and hard. The gate is now in a museum in Berlin.

Potters were probably the first people to use their skills to escape farm labour

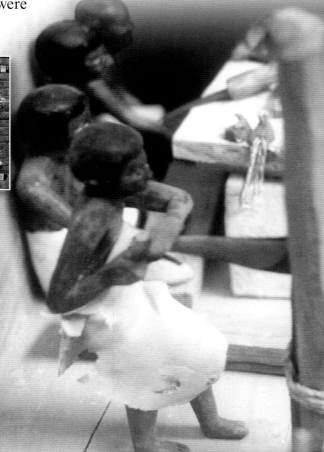

The beginning of crafts

The people who left the farms became craft workers. We know that some of them were potters, because pieces of the clay containers they made have survived. Others almost certainly made beautiful and useful things from leather and wood, but these fragile materials have vanished.

▲ **Mesopotamian gold**
As work became more specialized (divided into separate trades), only the wealthy could afford the finest crafts. Gold helmets like this one from Mesopotamia needed expensive materials and great skill to make. Only the country's rulers would have had one.

◀ **Carpenters at work**
We must guess about the lives of the first craftsmen and women, but we know much more about craft work in Ancient Egypt. There, wealthy people were buried with doll-like wooden figures to aid them in the afterlife in which they expected to be reborn. The tiny wooden carpenters in this workshop are using perfectly detailed tools like those used in life.

Be Free of
Work – be a Scribe

BRAIN-WORK OR HAND-WORK? The choice began with the development of writing, about 5,000 years ago in the Middle East. There, in the Nile river valley, people who could read and write were called scribes. Thanks to their skills, they paid no taxes – and never dirtied their hands with hard labour.

Scribes didn't do just desk jobs. They were clerks and officials. They measured fields and collected taxes. They organized the building of everything from a humble canal to a giant pyramid.

Scribes as overseers ▲
Wealthy Egyptians had the walls of their tombs painted with scenes from everyday life. In the middle of this farming picture, a scribe is giving orders with an outstretched finger. The weary field labourers obey him, working hard in the hot Egyptian sun.

Writing with reeds ▼
Scribes did their work using reeds chewed to make a brush or cut across for a pen. This beautiful reed case would have been the prized possession of a wealthy scribe. He would have mixed his inks on the ivory palette below.

An Egyptian scribe's tools

Scribe or bricklayer

To persuade his son to study hard, scribe Dua-Khety compared a scribe's work to every other trade. Of a bricklayer's job, he wrote, "he must work outside naked, kneading excrement to make bricks, then eat bread – without washing his hands."

Scribe in training

Becoming a scribe was not easy. Egyptians wrote using hieroglyphs – tiny pictures that stood for words or letters, sometimes both. Writing even a simple sentence meant learning hundreds of them. Student scribes practised writing with endless dull copying. They learned phrases that praised a scribe's life, such as "No job is free of supervisors, except the scribe's: he is the boss!"

◀ **Picture-writing**

For their "paperwork", scribes used papyrus – spongy reed hearts plaited and pressed into thin sheets. This one shows women with offerings for the goddess Hathor. In the hieroglyphic writing along the top, the pictures are read top to bottom. Rounded boxes, called cartouches, contain kings' names.

Ancient Egyptian papyrus

Scribe at work ▶

This wooden figure of a scribe shows him in a working pose, with a scroll (roll) of papyrus spread out across his knees. This model is called a ushabti. Ushabtis were placed in tombs to act as servants in the afterlife that Egyptians believed awaited them when they died.

9

Unfree Worlds

Slave market ▲
You could buy slaves at auction, like furniture. In Rome's markets, slaves wore wooden neck-tags describing them, to help buyers choose. The feet of newly captured slaves were dusted with chalk to show that they might be rebellious.

HOW WOULD YOU FEEL if your boss didn't pay you for the work you did, could sell you to another employer and even have the right to kill you for making only the slightest error? For slaves in Ancient Greece and Rome, all this was normal. Slaves were the possessions of their employers, just like a horse or ox.

House slave or manual labour ▲ ▶
Young, attractive or educated slaves were employed in homes as servants or teachers (above). Usually well treated, they could live better than the poorest free men and women. Farm slaves, like the labourers harvesting olives shown on the vase, mostly had a worse time. Many died of overwork, beatings or hunger.

● ● ● ● ● ● ● ● ● ● ● ● ● ● ● ● ●

Most slaves were captured in wars, but some were born to slave parents or sold themselves to pay debts. A lucky few bought or won their freedom. The rest spent their whole lives doing dirty, tiring jobs that nobody else wanted to do.

Greek slaves were cheap: the price tag was no more than the slave's food and housing for a year

Slave ship ▼

In the 16th and 17th centuries, slaves pulled the oars of Christian and Muslim galleys (rowed warships) fighting for control of the Mediterranean. Though Hollywood epics like *Ben Hur* (below) show slaves rowing Roman galleys, the crews of the Ancient world were actually paid free men.

Would You Believe . . . ?

Revolting slaves

Occasionally, slaves fought back. In the most famous Roman revolt of 73 BCE, slave-gladiator Spartacus led an army of 140,000 escaped slaves. When the army crushed the revolt, 6,000 slaves were crucified (executed on crosses) on the main road into Rome.

Elevated slaves

Roman slaves who won freedom could rise to positions of great wealth. Later, even those still enslaved were able to improve their status. When the Ayyubid dynasty ruled the Middle East in the 12th and 13th centuries, Mamluk slaves became a privileged class that the free fought to join.

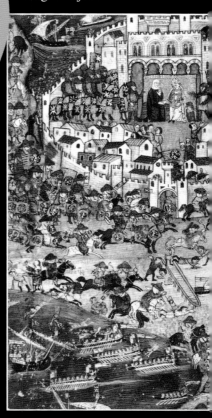

Mamluks seize Tripoli ▲

Captured as children and raised as Muslim warriors, Mamluk slaves were trusted in a time of treachery. By 1250, Mamluks ruled Egypt. Forty years later, they captured Tripoli, ending 200 years of Christian rule of the Holy Land.

Medieval Mystery

THE PEASANT FARMERS of Europe in the Middle Ages (500–1500 CE) were not slaves, but they weren't quite free either. Called serfs, they worked on their master's estate and received land to cultivate themselves. They had to get permission, and pay a fine, to move away or marry someone they chose.

Craft workers were paid. They could choose where they lived, their masters – and their wives or husbands. They were also protected by guilds. These trade associations stopped anyone who had not served an apprenticeship from working.

Three herrings and a loaf of bread – possible wages for a day's harvesting

Payment in goods ▶
As well as land, serfs got paid in goods. A day's harvesting might earn supper for the family. Sometimes, chance decided pay. For cutting hay, peasants on one English manor got as much of it as they could tie in a bundle and lift on a scythe.

Tradesmen at work ▶
Medieval craft workers learned the secret skills and techniques of a trade in an apprenticeship. During this seven-year training they lived with a master craftsman who taught them. At the end of their apprenticeship, they had to make a "masterpiece", which proved their skill at the craft and allowed them to join the craft guild.

Tailor

Hatter

Potter

A baker is punished for cheating

A priest gives last rites to plague victims

◀ **Crooked traders**
Tradesmen who cheated their customers were punished and humiliated. Bakers whose loaves were too small were dragged through the streets with the evidence tied round their necks.

The Black Death ▲
A disease called the Black Death swept through Europe in the 14th century. There was no cure, and blessings from priests (above) didn't help. A third of the population died, but the survivors demanded better wages paid in money.

◀ **Rebellious peasants**
Peasants revolted against the rules, fines and poverty of the manor. Labour shortages after the Black Death gave them more power. Rulers such as Sweden's Gustave Vasa (left) put down the revolts, but they could not stop them. By 1600 there were no serfs in England.

Death, revolt and freedom

A medieval saying claimed "towns make men free", and country serfs envied their town cousins. When epidemics killed half Europe's people, the surviving peasants wanted the same freedom as townspeople.

For the survivors, the Black Death was a blessing: wages tripled after the epidemic

Lock maker

Saddler

Weaver

Bookbinder

Joiner

The First Factories

Water power ▲
Water wheels were traditionally used to turn grind-stones in flour mills. Then, from 1769, they were used to power yarn-spinning machines.

S PLASHING AND DASHING through green countryside, rivers and streams seem like places to rest and relax. Yet 250 years ago, waterside factories powered a revolution in work. Their water wheels drove machines to make cloth, putting traditional weavers and spinners out of business.

These craft workers made thread and cloth by hand at home. But new looms and "spinning frames" invented in the 18th century were too big to work by hand so factories replaced craft workshops.

◀ Home to factory
Using machines like this, home workers spun threads from plant or animal fibres. Spinning wheels, and the looms that wove cloth, fitted easily into homes. Water-powered spinning machines did not!

▼ Town and factory
At day's end, a flood of workers left factories, often returning to homes built by the mill owner. Whole communities grew up around big factories like this one, which made sewing machines.

Hardships and benefits
Factory work was boring and often dangerous, and the hours were long. The towns that grew up around factories were unhealthy places, but it wasn't all bad news. Factory-made goods were cheaper than hand-made ones, and if all the family worked they earned more than before.

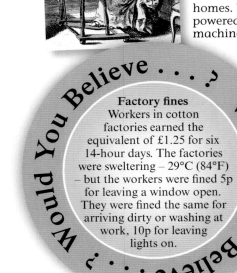

Would You Believe . . . ?

Factory fines
Workers in cotton factories earned the equivalent of £1.25 for six 14-hour days. The factories were sweltering – 29°C (84°F) – but the workers were fined 5p for leaving a window open. They were fined the same for arriving dirty or washing at work, 10p for leaving lights on.

Industrial iron ▶

The first English cloth factories helped
to start an Industrial Revolution, which
picked up speed with improvements in
shaping iron. Metal-working factories
were hellish places, glowing red-hot, as
German artist Adolph Menzel showed
in his picture *The Iron-Rolling Mill*.

▼ Children working

Factory owners could pay children less
than adults, so they employed workers
as young as five. Crawling under the
machines to clean, many children lost
their limbs and lives. This girl is in a
spinning room in a US factory in 1908.

15

Profession
or Trade?

CALLING A GENTLEMAN idle in the Middle Ages was a compliment. He would have been insulted if someone had called him hard-working. In those days, only common people worked at a trade. There were a few exceptions: it was respectable for a man to work in a profession.

"Profession" was the name given to three or four special jobs that needed long study ending with a difficult test. Lawyers, doctors, priests and often army and navy officers were called professionals.

Lord and master ▲
For noblemen such as this 13th-century German lord, Henry III of Meissen, work was for lesser people. When not ruling or riding to battle, he indulged in costly pleasures, such as hunting with hawks.

◄ Settling accounts
Wealthy, well-born people had to deal with merchants, like this one adding up a bill in 18th-century Japan. They would never marry their daughters to them. "He's in trade" meant "He's too common."

Until nursing became a profession in the 19th century, many nurses were drunks and lived by selling hospital drugs

Would You Believe . . . ?

Buying your way in
Success in the army required only money – officers' jobs were for sale. England's Duke of Wellington had no military training. He had never fought a battle when, in 1794, he bought the rank of colonel and led a regiment against the French.

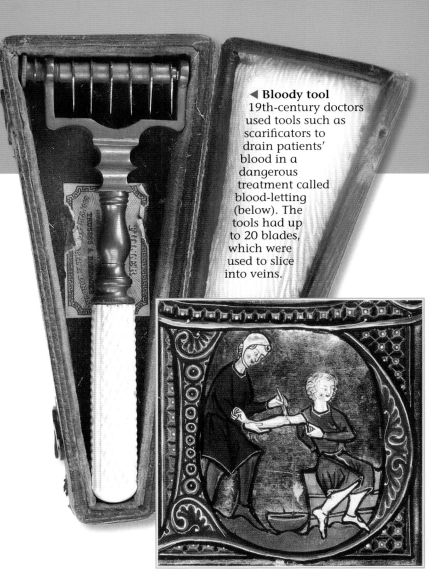

◀ Bloody tool
19th-century doctors used tools such as scarificators to drain patients' blood in a dangerous treatment called blood-letting (below). The tools had up to 20 blades, which were used to slice into veins.

Jobs for second sons

Traditionally, the wealth of families passed to the eldest son when the father died. Other sons received little and they worked in professions to earn a living. Daughters were expected to marry. Professions were closed to them until the late 19th century.

Blood-letting ▲
Blood-letting was popular from Ancient times. A high fever was thought to be caused by too much blood, so doctors opened their patients' veins to drain out some of it.

By the end of the 19th century, many more trades, such as teaching and nursing had become professions. Today there is no shame in working, and "professional" no longer has the same status. It has come to describe a job that anyone can do after a little training.

New professions

To become a professional doctor, architect or engineer, you need years of training. But the meaning of "professional" is changing. Now you can be a professional simply by earning money from what you do.

Skin care ▼
The work of a professional beauty therapist is not something most of us would try on ourselves. However, it's not as tricky as medicine or dentistry. Gaining a certificate in dermabrasion takes a couple of days.

Bake like a pro ▲
Hiring a professional cake decorator should bring you a stunning result. In this and many other trades, being professional means having high standards of skill and dealing with customers in a business-like way.

Up the Workers

Work wounds ▲
An unguarded machine in a US factory tore off this worker's arm and broke his leg in 1908. The factory owner paid nothing. Union pressure has led to better factory safety and forced employers to pay compensation after accidents.

FREED FROM SLAVERY AND SERFDOM, workers could pick their masters, but it wasn't a real choice. With the growth of factories, jobs were badly paid, tiring and often dangerous. Gradually, skilled workers realized that by joining together they could bargain with employers to get better pay and conditions. So they formed groups called trade unions.

Workers went on strike (stopped work) to get better deals. Employers were furious, and Britain's parliament banned "unlawful combinations" of workers. But the union movement grew and the laws didn't last. Unions have since helped to improve pay and safety worldwide.

▼ Early union
In this annual march, people remember six farm workers who were punished for starting a union in 1834. Named after their Dorset village, the Tolpuddle Martyrs were banished to Australia. Their punishment started an outcry that helped unions to grow.

Would You Believe . . . ?

Fair pay for fair work
Employers fought to keep unions out of factories. US motor tycoon Henry Ford did so in an unusual way. In 1914, he doubled pay and cut daily working hours from nine to eight. Employees worked harder – and Ford's profits soared.

The hammer and sickle communist symbol represents farm and factory workers united.

Shared wealth

As unions grew, German writer Karl Marx suggested that workers should run all society, sharing out work and wealth between them. The idea of communist or socialist nations became a reality with revolutions in Russia (1917) and China (1949).

◀ **Heroic workers**
This 1935 poster makes the lives of Russian workers look happy and glorious. In fact, communists were no more successful at running farms and factories than private owners. Plagued by shortages and lack of political freedom, the communist experiment in Russia ended in 1991.

19

Unemployment
and Depression

WHAT'S WORSE THAN WORKING too hard? Not working at all! Unemployment happens when there are just too many workers chasing too few jobs. Those left without any work to do face living on benefits (payments from the government) at best, and hardship or hunger at worst.

When people stop buying, businesses make fewer things and need fewer workers. Sacked workers don't buy things because they have no money. This can lead to a slow-down of all business and work that we call a depression.

▲ **Black economy**
Unemployment forces many people to earn money out of sight in an "informal", "black" or "underground" economy. In the 1920s, these two men in the USA earned a living making alcohol, which was banned at the time.

Would You Believe . . . ?

Roman dole
Supporting unemployed workers with money or food has a long history. From 123 BCE, the rulers of Ancient Rome gave half-price corn to those without work. Later, those without work got free corn – with pork, olive oil, wine and even entertainment.

◄ **Depression victims**
Trade slumped worldwide in 1929, starting a 10-year depression. In the USA, a drought made life worse for farmers, driving many from their land. This fleeing family is about to sell their possessions to buy food.

Striking for jobs ▲
Workers get angry when companies sack them to make more money for themselves. When French car-maker Renault closed a plant (factory) in Belgium in 1997, work stopped at Renault plants all over Europe.

▶ Globalization protest
This banknote-covered monster devoured a globe in a 2009 protest against globalization. The protesters claimed that world leaders meeting nearby were plotting to protect the rich in a worsening depression, while the poor and unemployed suffered.

Boom or bust?
Work, sales and trade link countries together. In good times, this "globalization" can cut shop prices and help create work. But there's a catch. We may lose our jobs because people on the other side of the world no longer want what we make. In a depression, our global links spread unemployment and poverty further and faster than ever before.

● ● ● ● ● ● ● ● ● ● ● ●

Work without jobs ▼
Communities that produce all they need for themselves don't have employers, so they don't have unemployment either. The Akha people of Laos grow, spin, weave and wear their own cotton. But because they don't trade it, depressions pass them by.

Women's Work

Making wine in the Middle Ages

IN A CROWDED ROMAN arena, two gladiators fight. The crowd cheers as the winner bows – and lifts off *her* helmet. Female warriors shouldn't surprise us. Women have always worked, and not just in traditional jobs of cleaning and child care.

In ancient, distant societies, such as the Lenape (opposite), women were expected to do heavy work. In Medieval Europe, wives of craftsmen like blacksmiths worked with their husbands. Many continued in the trade if their husbands died.

Making wine ▲
Before factories and offices began, all indoor work was "housework". Medieval women prepared and preserved wine and beer. The female brewers of England were known as ale wives, and in London's Fleet Street, they controlled the brewing trade.

Would You Believe . . . ?

Scottish coal mining
In 1812, women miners of Scotland climbed a 36 m (117 ft) ladder carrying their own weight in coal more than 20 times a day. They might lift two tonnes of coal this way every day, until they were as much as 60 years old.

Women in charge ▶
The wives of medieval noblemen were administrators of huge, busy estates. While their husbands dabbled in politics and war, they organized everything made and traded on the manor. When their husbands were away, they were often left in charge of a castle and its lands.

◀ **Lenape women**
To the Lenape people who lived where New York now stands, farming was women's work. The men hunted and fished, but thought farming unmanly. Their "laziness" shocked European explorers in 1609.

Domestic service ▼
The daughters of the poor in 19th-century England became "domestics", cooking and cleaning for wealthier people. Even only moderately well-off families employed a cook and maids. Pay was poor, but servants were fed and housed.

Rolling pastry in a Victorian-style kitchen

Jobs for women

In Victorian England, women worked in only a few industries. These figures are from 1841.

Domestic service	447,606
Weaving	101,605
Dressmaking	70,518
Laundry	43,497
Teaching	27,754
Farm labouring	26,815
Cleaning	18,019
Sewing	15,680
Lace making	14,394
Farming	13,398
Nursing	12,476

Country girls who could not get work as servants faced a lifetime of back-breaking farm labour

23

Home or Career
... Why not Both?

WHEN WAR TORE THE WORLD apart in the 20th century, it also changed ideas about "women's work". As men became soldiers, their wives and mothers took jobs in farms and factories. When peace returned, women didn't want the undervalued, underpaid work they'd done before.

War wasn't the only reason why women demanded equality at work. Since the 19th century, universities had been open to them. Educated women didn't want second-class jobs.

For every pound, **dollar or euro a man earns, a woman doing the same job earns just** 84 pence **or cents**

Rosie the Riveter ▼
During World War II (1939–45), nations needed women to do jobs left vacant by soldiers. In the USA, Rosie the Riveter recruited factory workers. Her slogan "We can do it!" still encourages women to help each other.

Men don't do housework
Though women now have careers, studies show they still do three-quarters of the housework. Men *say* they share chores but actually do little. High pay helps women. Statistics show that for every £10,000 women earn, they do two hours less housework each week.

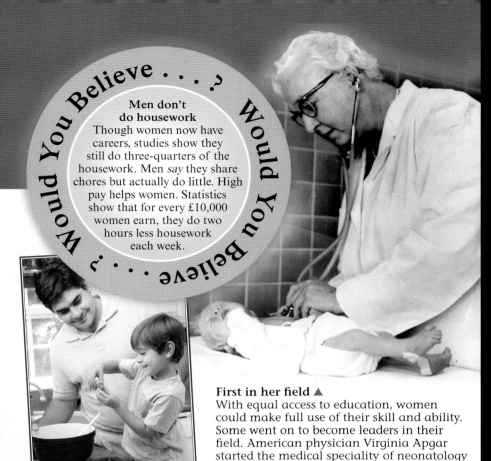

Top jobs

Today, the most important jobs in politics and business are no longer just for men. Women run publishing and banking empires and even nations. However, what makes these women special is how unusual they are. It's still mostly men at the top. Research shows that companies with women at the top do better, but an invisible barrier of prejudice nicknamed the "glass ceiling" keeps women in more junior jobs.

First in her field ▲
With equal access to education, women could make full use of their skill and ability. Some went on to become leaders in their field. American physician Virginia Apgar started the medical speciality of neonatology (the care of new-born babies).

Stay at home dads ▲
As more women join the workforce, some men move the other way. They give up their paid work to take on the jobs of bringing up kids and looking after the home – tasks once seen as women's work.

● ● ● ● ● ● ● ● ● ● ● ● ●

Working at home ▶
Changes in technology have made it much easier for women to have a career and look after the home and kids. Keeping in touch by internet and 'phone, they are often more productive than co-workers in offices. However, not all employers agree to "telecommuting".

Is equality real?

In the developed world, women have won equal employment rights. Many juggle successful careers with child care, but traditions change more slowly than laws. Women still hold fewer top jobs than men and earn less for the same work.

Politician ▲
Once called the most powerful woman in the world, Angela Merkel became Chancellor (leader) of Germany in 2005. She trained as a physicist but became involved in politics in 1989 as communist rule crumbled in her native East Germany and the country joined West Germany to form one nation. She is seen here talking to the French president Nicolas Sarkozy.

Working for Nothing

I T'S A JOB YOU'D THINK no-one would want: "Help needed. Unpredictable hours. Risk of death. No pay." Volunteer lifeboat crews and firefighters do jobs like this. Their only reward is the work itself. Volunteers don't just save lives. They're vital wherever money is scarce.

Volunteering began in the Middle Ages with religious charities and "good works" of the rich. Ever since, people have given their time to help those less fortunate than themselves: by teaching, feeding, nursing and protecting.

Underground railroad ▲
In 19th-century USA, people risked violence to help slaves from southern states escape to freedom in the north, where slavery was banned. The scheme was nicknamed the Underground Railway because its secret routes resembled a rail network.

Volunteer firefighters ▶
Nearly three-quarters of US firefighters are volunteers. Fire stations pay a few professionals, but the volunteers have other regular jobs. When the alarm sounds, they rush from their desks to help. More than 50 die each year fighting flames.

You can help
Volunteers are now more important than ever. Governments pay for only "essential" public service jobs. Volunteers do the rest. Students break their studies to experience "gap years". Other volunteers regularly give up weeks, days or hours and ask for nothing in return.

Rescue at sea ▶
British lifeboat crews rescue 150 people a week from the sea, often in dangerous storms. Only one in 20 is paid for risking their own life to save the lives of others.

Volunteers learn valuable job skills and their experiences help them to understand other people's problems

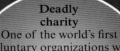

Would You Believe . . . ?

Deadly charity
One of the world's first voluntary organizations was Week's Charity, which was set up in the 15th century to supply faggots (bundles of sticks) for the burning alive of heretics (people who disagreed with the teachings of the Catholic Church).

Oil and feathers ▶
Washing seabirds, such as this guillemot that was caught in a spilled oil slick, is slow work. It wouldn't happen without volunteers. Most of the birds that survive the oil and the clean-up thrive when released.

Tsunami devastation ▲
When a tsunami hit Southeast Asia in 2004, offers of help overwhelmed relief organizers. The volunteers who travelled to devastated Sumatra (above) and elsewhere were mainly those with relief experience and specialist skills, and people who spoke local languages.

27

Modern
Slavery

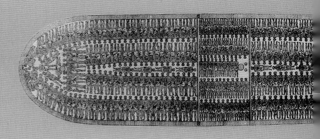

THE BUYING AND SELLING of workers should be ancient history, but it's not. In the 18th century, slaves had black skins, not white, and they worked in American and Caribbean plantations instead of Mediterranean olive groves. Cruelly treated, they were sometimes worked to death.

Eighteenth-century British slavers bought slaves in Africa and shipped them across the Atlantic. There they swapped them for sugar, which fetched a high price in England.

William Wilberforce, MP and abolitionist

Would You Believe . . . ? Would You Believe . . . ?

Bargain slaves
It's never been so cheap to buy another human being! According to campaign group Free the Slaves, slaves are sold today for as little as US $90. The cost of a slave in the American south in 1850 was the equivalent of US $40,000.

People for sale ▲
Between the 15th and 19th centuries, at least 12 million Africans were taken to America to be sold at auction, like this man. The chains and neck irons would have made work impossible, so slave owners used brutality and torture to enforce obedience.

Protesting against slavery ▲
Thanks to human rights campaigners, such as William Wilberforce, Britain banned slavery in 1807. Slavery continued elsewhere despite opposition from the Anti-Slavery Society, shown here meeting in 1840. It was banned in the USA in 1865.

◀ Slave ship
To save money on the Atlantic crossing, slaves were chained naked in the airless holds of ships, like sardines in cans. As many as one in ten people died during this "middle passage" to America.

◀ Domestic slavery
Each year, four million women become household slaves. Some are lured to Europe from developing nations with false promises of work and education. When they arrive, they are forced to work without pay.

After unloading sugar in England, ships loaded trade goods and returned to Africa, completing a triangular route. The cruel exchange of people for goods was nicknamed the "triangular trade".

● ● ● ● ● ● ● ● ● ● ● ● ● ● ●

The end of slavery?
Slavery is illegal everywhere today, but it still happens. People are trapped into slavery using debt. Their wages are so low that they will never repay what they owe. They work in fields, hotels, factories and homes – perhaps even in your neighbourhood.

Modern debt slavery ▶
Brazilian farmers are planting vast sugar cane fields. Penniless workers enslaved by debt, like this man, cut the crop. Overcharged for housing, food and transport, they cannot escape and are sometimes worked to death.

● ● ● ● ● ● ● ● ● ●

Today at least 27 million people are still kept as prisoners and forced to work for no pay

Not too Young
to go to Work

CHILDREN IN THE PAST worked as soon as they could stand. Toddlers yelled at birds in medieval fields to stop them eating crops. Older kids picked slugs from growing plants. 19th-century children worked up hot chimneys and down dark mines.

Picking berries ▶
It's no coincidence that there are long school holidays in summer. This is the busiest time on farms, and children have traditionally helped out with the harvest. Their small hands mean they are better than adults at some tasks. This 10-year-old American girl is picking fruit in 1910.

◀ **Cheap tea**
Child labour in the developing world means bargains in our shops. Employers pay children less than adults and pass the savings on to customers who buy what they make. If we were willing to pay more for a cuppa, this 10-year-old girl in Nepal would not have to pick tea.

A young Nepalese girl picks tea quickly with both hands

218 million children around the world work to support their families, often in very dangerous jobs

◄ Paper round

Part-time jobs are a good way to boost pocket money, but labour laws limit what you can do. In the UK, you must be over the age of 14 to work in a paid job. Local governments decide how many hours you can work.

Tyre repair ►

Full-time jobs harm children, ending their education and sometimes damaging their health. In poorer nations, labour laws are hard to enforce and child labour is common. This youngster is repairing tyres in The Gambia.

Today, kids in country areas still sometimes skip school to pick crops, but make up the time later. Less fortunate children work *instead of* studying. Their families are so poor they need the money a child can earn.

Child soldiers

When war breaks out, children can find themselves in nightmare jobs. Often enlisted at gunpoint, they become the foot soldiers of rebel armies. In Sudan, Congo, Somalia, Colombia and Sri Lanka, rebels recruited boys as soon as they were strong enough to fire a gun.

Militia volunteer ▲
When the USA fought to control the Southeast Asian country of Vietnam during the 1960s and 70s, a communist guerrilla army resisted its attacks. The guerrillas recruited children to fight for them. The weapon on the shoulder of this 12-year-old recruit fires grenades.

Working Hours,
Days or Months

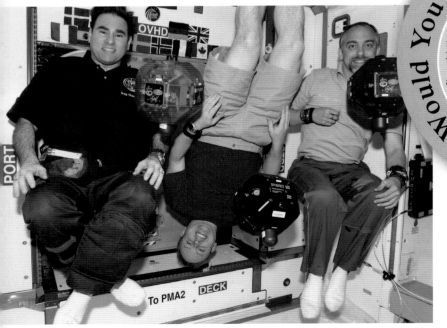

Fishy business ▲
Fishing boats such as this trawler may sail for days before the crew can start work. When the trawler reaches a shoal of fish, the crew don't rest much because the more fish they catch, the more money they earn. The very long hours help to make working at sea in the fishing industry one of the world's most dangerous jobs.

WILL IT BE NINE TO FIVE OR 24/7? Your working day could be either of these – and anything in between. How long you work depends on what you do and where you do it. Most office staff in Europe and the USA expect to be at work for no more than eight hours each day, Monday to Friday.

For a few of us though, working days stretch out far beyond these limits. Keeping vital services running may mean staff have to work much longer hours. And if you're in orbit around Earth, you can't just hang up your space suit and go home.

Would You Believe . . . ? Would You Believe . . . ?

Dozy doctors
To save money, many hospitals make trainee doctors regularly attend work for at least 24 hours without a break. By the end of a day and a night, they are exhausted. Patients they treat are eight times more likely to die than those treated by doctors working normal hours.

◄ Astronauts
Imagine leaving for work and not going home again for six months. For astronauts on the International Space Station, that's perfectly normal. Their working days are weird too, since they can watch the sun rise 'in the morning' every 90 minutes.

◀ No time off
The Christian warriors who fought to capture the Holy Land in the First Crusade (1096) didn't return home for more than three years. Just capturing the city of Antioch (left) took them eight months.

◀ Tour of duty
This soldier returning from the battlefield is seeing his seven-month-old son for the first time. Warfare continues day and night, so normal rules about working hours can't apply in the armed forces.

Work to live or live to work?

Laws limiting working hours save the rest of us from exhaustion, but we're lucky. Two centuries ago, workers had no protection. Six-day weeks and 12-hour days were common – as they still are in much of the developing world.

Night shift ▼
Services such as rail networks need staff 24 hours a day. They employ workers in shifts, of maybe eight hours each, so that some work nights and weekends. Shift work disrupts workers' sleep and leisure and damages their health.

Night work **may cause cancer: no wonder those who do it call it the** graveyard shift

Dangerous
and Deadly

THE NIGHT BEGAN LIKE EVERY other for the miners of Hebi pit in China's Henan province. They started the exhausting work of hewing filthy black coal. But, for 34 of them, it would be the last shift they ever worked, because on that night in 2005, an explosion ripped through the mine.

Although a Chinese mine is the world's most hazardous place to work, other jobs are almost as risky. Fishermen, lumberjacks and building workers face death or injury daily. Risk isn't always obvious: farming and rubbish collection are near the top of the world's danger list.

Construction workers ▲
Each year, one in every 2,000 building workers dies, making building the fourth most dangerous job. In the early 1900s, when this picture was taken, Mohawk people famously walked the high girders of scaffolding on New York skyscrapers. To them, the danger was an attraction: it showed off their bravery.

Mining in China ▼
These rescuers went down Hebi mine in search of survivors of the explosion on 3 October, 2005. The blast had killed half the miners. Two months earlier, the Chinese government had stopped mine managers from investing in their own mines because they were ignoring safety measures to increase production.

Clearing land-mines ▲
Planted during wars to blow up troops who stand on them, land-mines are still deadly when peace returns. Finding and removing them is slow, dangerous work, but if de-miners follow safety rules, their job is no more dangerous than working on a building site.

Most accidents **happen when workers are tired,** ignore safety rules **or are** driven to meet targets

Dangerous entertaining

Circus audiences gasp at the risks that high-wire artists, fire-eaters and lion tamers take. However, they rarely see the real hazards. Mauling by a jungle beast is rare: animal trainers are at greater risk from lifting heavy objects and from their animals' diseases.

Would You Believe . . . ?

Deadly driving

What's more dangerous than working? Driving a car. Most workers are safer at work than they are when they are driving to get there. And can you guess what is the most deadly threat in the most dangerous occupations? That's right – traffic accidents!

◄ Lumberjack

Forest work is four times more dangerous than most industrial work. Falling objects cause two in three accidents, saws just one in fifty. Loggers have more accidents if they skip breakfast and drink lots of coffee, making them tired and careless.

Not to be tried at home ▲

Big-top performers protect themselves with simple actions. Fire-eaters lick their lips and wire-walkers carry things to help them balance. Despite these techniques, accidents are common. You must never try tricks without training.

Revolting Careers

YEUCH! YOU DO WHAT?!
No matter how much technology cleans up our world, there will always be some revolting work that nobody wants. In India, there is even a caste (class) of people who have traditionally done these horrible jobs. Called Dalits (ground-down people), they include cemetery workers, sewer cleaners and leather workers.

In the past, there were far more stinky, slimy tasks than there are now. In Ancient Rome, vomit catchers were employed at banquets for queasy guests. In 18th-century London, "night-soil men" emptied overflowing lavatories.

Greenbottle fly ▶

▼ **Blowfly larva**

▲ **Body farmers**
Judging when a murder victim died is impossible if we don't know how human bodies decay. So forensic anthropologists leave corpses to rot, then look at the insects that swarm around them. Eggs, maggots and flies give them a grisly but precise calendar.

◀ **Sewer cleaner**
Dalits such as this sewer worker in Mumbai, India, not only do the country's essential but disgusting tasks, they also face prejudice and sometimes violence. Other castes see their work as "impure", although Indian law gives Dalits equal rights.

◀ ▶ The dirty Middle Ages
Medieval tanners (far left) stank of the skins of dead animals they made into leather, softening the hides with dog poo. Bath-house owners (left) removed fleas and blackheads, and corpse carriers (right) buried the blistered bodies when the Black Death killed one-third of the population.

Out of sight
Dirty jobs have not disappeared. Improved sewers flush away human waste hygienically, but we still need workers to deal with dead bodies and to clean up after the messy, smelly and untidy. Most of these workers do their jobs out of sight and almost forgotten by those who benefit.

▼ Sniff this
At deodorant companies, odour judges test new products by sniffing smelly armpits so you don't have to. And it gets worse. They also sniff bad breath, smelly feet, cat litter and nappies.

Workers in stinky jobs only notice the smell on returning from holiday

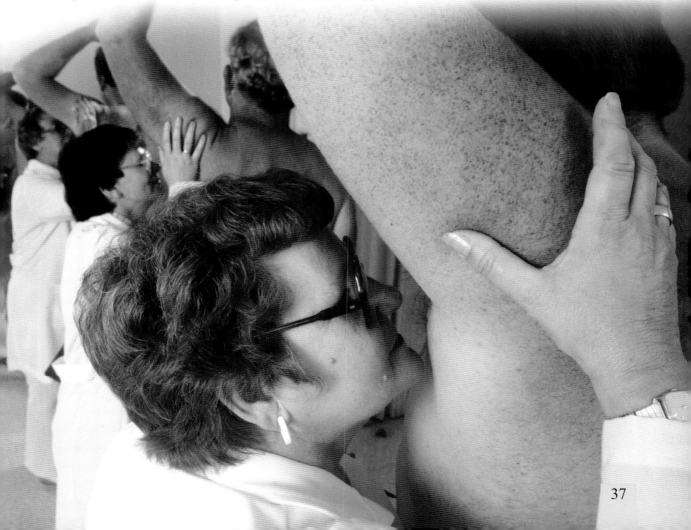

Jammy Jobs

Plastic brick heaven ▼
All four LEGO® theme parks employ designers and builders who work to repair and renew models. It can be cold, wet work – modelling doesn't stop in bad weather.

THE GOOD NEWS ABOUT your dream job is that it really does exist. Whether your fantasy work involves drawing cartoons, eating chocolate, making models in LEGO® bricks or watching TV, there *really are* companies that will pay you to do exactly that. The bad news is that you face stiff competition – everybody is after the same job.

▲ Bed tester
Snoozing is all part of the job if you are a bed tester for a hotel chain, but there's more to it than that. The Director of Sleep checks everything that might keep guests awake, from astrological signs to paint colours.

Fortunately, there are things you can do to improve your chances of success in your dream career. Education helps. To become a chocolate taster, start by studying food science. Experience is important too, so take a photo of your best LEGO® models before you break them up.

▼ Looking after an island
Imagine waking up to this view. Ben Southall does just that after beating 35,000 other applicants for the job of caretaker of Hamilton Island on Australia's Great Barrier Reef. His "chores" include feeding fish, SCUBA diving, hiking – and blogging about the job.

When one choc taster for a posh London store quit, she said, "It's a horrible job. I wouldn't recommend it."

Real-life Willy Wonka ▶
Chocolate tasters usually have other jobs in the factory and spend just part of their time comparing samples. Most taste and spit to avoid getting fat. Tasting booths have red lighting to change the look of the chocolates and stop appearance from influencing the tasters' opinion.

The drawbacks
Be careful what you wish for! Something you enjoy can easily become a tedious chore when you *have* to do it every day, whether you want to or not. And what could be worse than becoming the assistant to your favourite film star, only to discover she's a monster!

Would You Believe . . . ?

Work or play?
Playing computer games for a living sounds fun. But for Chinese "gold farmers" who build up skill levels for characters in games like *World of Warcraft*, it's hell. Paid as little as 30p (50 cents) an hour, they work 10-hour days, sleeping and eating in small offices.

High Days
and Holidays

A LIFE WITHOUT WORK MAY seem like an impossible dream, but once, it was normal. People from the distant past, who lived by hunting and collecting food, often did not understand the difference between work and leisure. They may not even have had a word in their language that meant "work".

Roman holidays ▲
The Romans, shown here honouring the goddess Ceres, knew how to enjoy themselves. Leaders eager for popularity declared more and more public holidays, so that by 1000 CE, Romans worked only every other day.

Yanomami ▼
For these Amazon rainforest people, work and play blend together. They do not use money because the forest provides all their needs. Adults spend fewer than four hours a day doing what we would call work – some of it hunting and fishing.

Would You Believe . . . ? Would You Believe . . . ?

Holiday reasons
Days when people stopped work in Ancient Rome included the weekend (every eight days), birthday of a god, anniversary of a Roman army defeat or victory, gladiator match, holiday for a forgotten reason, or just because it was an unlucky day to do business.

Boredom drives many lottery winners to return to their old jobs

Most of us know only too well what work is. We even have a word for "no work". We call it a holiday. Holidays began as "holy days" when religion demanded believers rest and worship. Today, we still celebrate these festivals, even if we forget their religious beginnings.

Tokyo crowds ▶
Shoved into crowded trains, Japanese office staff are pushed around at work too. Few dare to take all the holiday they are allowed, in case their bosses think they are slacking. Some work 21-hour days when they are busy. Worried about overwork, the Japanese government can force workers to take time off.

▲ Thanksgiving
The turkey is a symbol of the American holiday of Thanksgiving. This began as a Christian festival, giving thanks to God. But for most Americans today, it's just a family get-together and a chance to feast.

No more work

A few lucky people win enough money in lotteries to make their life one long holiday – but hardly any of them take this opportunity. Two-thirds of lottery winners stay in their jobs. Some work part-time or start their own business. Only one in seven gives up work altogether.

Luxury leisure ▼
Lottery winners who dream of a life of leisure on a luxury yacht quickly discover that their jackpot doesn't go far. Boats like this one can cost £5 million (US$8.25 million) to buy, and the same to run for ten years. Only the biggest winners can afford them.

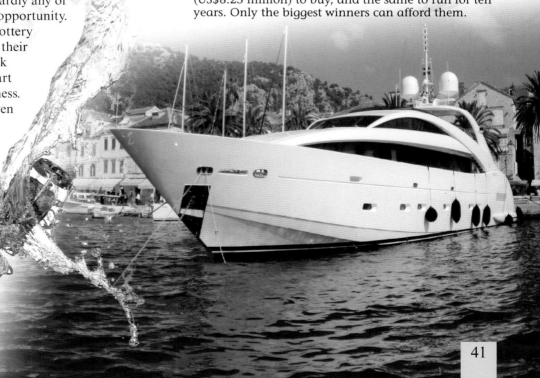

Machines
that Work

ROBOTS SURROUND US, BUT WE HAVE BECOME
so used to their company that we barely notice them any more.
Laundry robots wash and dry our clothes; kitchen robots
clean our dishes. They are not as glamorous as the walking, talking,
wise-cracking robots of the movies, but they
certainly take the "work" out of housework.

Automatic servants

Robots are machines that do
the work we can't do – or don't
want to do. They repeat the same
task endlessly, without tiring
or complaining. They work in
conditions that would kill us and
carry out tasks more precisely
than any expert human could.

I, Robot ▼
Actor Will Smith
battles against
two-legged servant
robots in this
Hollywood fantasy
set in 2035. In real
life, just walking
upright is so difficult
that robots that do it
can rarely do much else.

Would You Believe . . . ?

Robot chess
As early as 1770,
a chess-playing "robot"
amazed people in Europe
and America. It beat even the
scientist and statesman Benjamin
Franklin. A life-size figure, "the
Turk", played at a board on top
of a cogwheel-filled box. In
fact, the box hid an expert
chess player who made
the moves.

One of the first robots, in 1738, was a mechanical duck that ate, drank and left realistic droppings

Early home help ▲
Inventors quickly gave up any hope of building all-purpose home robots. Instead, they concentrated on labour-saving machines that did just one task and did it well. This advertisement for a primitive washing machine and wringer appeared in the 1870s.

Roomba – a robot that cleans floors

Scientific robots

Much scientific research involves doing the same task over and over again. Robots are increasingly taking over this boring work. For example, decoding DNA, nature's "building plan", is now done entirely automatically. Robots also quickly test thousands of chemical combinations to find the most useful.

Robots do their work best when their tasks are carefully organized for them, as on a factory production line. They can't cope with chaos. Something as simple as a closed door, for example, stops a robot floor cleaner like Roomba in its tracks.

▲ Tireless factory slave
Robots began to do the most boring factory jobs in the early 1960s. Today, a million are at work around the world, mostly in car and electronics factories. Factories in Japan have more robots than any other nation, but even there, human workers still outnumber robots by nearly 320 to 1.

Robotic surgery ▲
In the operating theatre, this Da Vinci robot can carry out heart surgery or a hundred other surgical procedures. Though it is guided by a human surgeon, it can make cuts more accurately than any human hand.

Swarm robots ▶
Robotics experts have studied birds and insects to give their machines more intelligence. Working in "swarms", these small, cheap robots can work together to perform tasks that would defeat one larger one. Members of the swarm communicate with each other to get the job done, just as ants leave scent trails to lead their comrades to food.

Workforce of the Future?

THE END OF WORK ALWAYS seems to be just around the corner. In 1936, a journalist suggested that 30 years later "... work will be limited to three hours a day". The rise of robots in the 1980s made others predict that future factories would work in darkness, without human staff.

"Lights-out" factories are a reality today, but they are rare. And though machines and computers have certainly reduced the amount of hard work there is to do, they have also created new tasks that only humans can complete.

◄ **Safe hands**
Robots' clumsy reputation has kept them out of jobs that need a "human touch". That could soon change. The Shadow robot hand mimics the human hand exactly. Pressure sensors built into its "skin" enable the hand to pick up objects as fragile as a light bulb.

Different jobs

Today, many people are doing jobs that didn't exist 25 years ago – such as website designer. Technology is changing so fast that predicting what jobs we will all be doing in another quarter of a century is all but impossible. One thing seems certain though: we won't all be living lives of leisure while machines do the work for us.

Many people who have jobs feel that they must work harder than ever to keep up with robots

Find out More

You can find out lots more about the history of work from these websites and places to visit.

Websites

Be your own boss
www.pbs.org/teachers/connect/resources/3476/preview
It sounds easy, but can you make it work?

The butcher, the baker and candle maker
www.museumoflondon.org.uk/English/EventsExhibitions/Permanent/medieval/Games/Apprentice.htm
Go to church, get an education, work your socks off and know your place in medieval England.

The American work ethic
www.knowitall.org/kidswork/index.html
Play games and learn about glamorous jobs in a TV studio, theatre and hospital in *Kids Work Town*.

You too could be a mill owner
www.mylearning.org/intermediate-interactive.asp?type=4&journeyid=160
Spot the latest trends in 19th-century woollen manufacturing and become a millionaire.

Robot bomb squad
www.pbs.org/wgbh/nova/robots
Choose the right robot for the job and watch it get to work.

Be a scribe
www.pbs.org/teachers/connect/resources/51/preview
Click on Rameses Records History to watch a reconstruction of scribes at work.

Flies and corpses
www.pbs.org/wnet/nature/episodes/crime-scene-creatures/interactive-determine-the-time-of-death/4390
Learn how a forensic entomologist uses insects to find out the time of death in this interactive game.

Places to visit

National Coal Mining Museum for England
Caphouse Colliery, New Road, Overton
Wakefield WF4 4RH
Telephone: 01924 848806
Website: www.ncm.org.uk
Descend 140m (460ft) down one of Britain's oldest working mines. There's lots to see above ground too, including the 1876 steam winder and the stables, where you can meet the pit ponies.

Lanhydrock
Bodmin, Cornwall PL30 5AD
Telephone: 01208 265950
Website: www.nationaltrust.org.uk/main/w-lanhydrock
A rare picture of life below stairs in the 19th century. Kitchens, dairy, bakery and bedrooms are some of the servants' quarters on view.

Quarry Bank Mill and Styal Estate
Styal, Wilmslow, Cheshire SK9 4LA
Telephone: 01625 445896
Website: www.nationaltrust.org.uk/main/w-quarrybankmillandstyalestate
Watch – and hear – the huge looms at work in this restored 18th-century cotton mill. Shiver with cold in the Apprentice House while you learn about the lives of the children who worked here.

Watford Fire Museum
Fire Station, Whippendell Road Junction, Rickmansworth Road, Watford, Hertfordshire
Telephone: 01923 232297 (Watford Museum)
Website: www.watfordmuseum.org.uk/firemuseum
Fire service equipment, uniform and photographs. Based in the old workshops of Watford fire station, this museum is looked after by two former fire officers and has limited opening times.

St Fagans National History Museum
Cardiff CF5 6XB
Telephone: 02920 573500
Website: www.museumwales.ac.uk/en/stfagans
An open-air museum with more than 40 buildings including a tannery, working blacksmith's forge, weaver, miller and baker.

Glossary

Did you read anything you didn't understand? Some of the more complicated and unusual terms used in this book are explained here.

Babylon
Powerful city that grew up between the Tigris and Euphrates rivers in what is now Iraq, some 4,000 years ago.

communist
Someone who believes in the fair distribution of wealth and an equal chance for all.

craft
Skilled work making useful or beautiful things with hand tools.

Crusades
Campaigns in the 11th–13th centuries by Christian soldiers to free the Holy Land of Palestine from Muslim rule.

debt
Money that must be repaid.

depression
A time when business activity slows down and workers have no jobs.

employee
Someone who does work and is paid money for it.

employer
A person or company that provides work and pays money to those who do it.

estate
Large area of land, often used for farming or hunting.

globalization
The linking of every country's trade in a vast network controlled by a few businesses.

guerilla
Volunteer soldier who fights outside a regular army, often in a revolution or for a cause in which they strongly believe.

guild
Organization of craft workers in the Middle Ages, which aimed to protect their skills and jobs.

hieroglyph
Word or sound-sign in a system of picture writing.

Industrial Revolution
Period in the 18th and 19th centuries when machines replaced craft workers, and improvements in transport and farming changed people's lives in Europe and North America.

Mesopotamia
Ancient land spreading between the Mediterranean Sea and the Gulf, now mostly Iraq.

Middle Ages
The period of European history between ancient and modern times: roughly CE 500–1500.

Middle East
Region of the world bordered by three continents of Europe, Asia and Africa.

production line
Where workers do just one task in the making of a product that moves along the line, emerging complete at the end.

profession
In the past, the respectable job of lawyer, doctor or priest; today, any job requiring a skill or training.

revolt
Strong protest in which people refuse to obey their rulers or those who give them orders.

serf
Slave of the Middle Ages, who worked on their owner's land in exchange for the right to farm a small plot for their family.

shift work
Work done at inconvenient times, or over longer periods than normal daytime work.

tax
Money paid to a government so that it can provide necessary services for everyone, such as education and transport.

trade union
Modern workers' organization that aims to protect the jobs and safety of its members.

volunteer
Someone who chooses to work for the benefit of others, for little or no reward.

wage
Money paid for work done, especially if paid at the end of each week, in cash.

Index

Acknowledgements

The publisher would like to thank the following for their kind permission to reproduce their photographs:

Position key: c=centre; b=bottom; left=left; r=right; t=top

Cover: Punchstock

1c: Andrea Leone/Shutterstock; 4tc: Simon A Weber/iStockphoto; 4tr: Chris Schmidt/iStockphoto; 5bc: James Boardman/Alamy; 5tr: Lisa F. Young/iStockphoto; 6bc: Ann Ronan Picture Library/Heritage Image Partnership; 6cl: Josep Renalias/Wikipedia; 7tr: The Print Collector/Alamy; 8c: Robert Harding World Imagery/Corbis; 8cr: Janne Ahvo/iStockphoto; 9cr: Mannel Velasco/iStockphoto; 9br: Z.Radovan/Lebrecht; 9tl: Maugli/Shutterstock; 10cl: North Wind Pictures Archives/Alamy; 10br: Photos 12/Alamy; 12c: Nikolay Suslow/iStockphoto; 12tc: Ints Vikmanis/iStockphoto; 12cr: Philip Lange/iStockphoto; 14br: Mary Evans Picture Library/Alamy; 14tc: iStockphoto; 17br: Artak Ayvazyan/iStockphoto; 17cr: David H. Lewis/iStockphoto; 17tc: Wellcome Library, London; 18bc: Nigel Housden/Alamy/Alamy; 18c: Majoros Laszio/iStockphoto; 19cl: Swim Ink 2, LLC, Corbis; 19tr: Karl Thaller/iStockphoto; 20bl: Library of Congress; 20tr: Library of Congress; 21tl: Bernard Bisson/Sygma/Corbis; 21bc: Gideon Mendel/Corbis; 22br: Rue Des Archives; 23br: Wales Heritage Photos/Alamy; 24bc: Bettmann/Corbis; 24c: iStockphoto; 25cr: Vario Images GmbH & Co.KG/Alamy; 25bc: Don Bayley/iStockphoto; 25cl: iStockphoto; 26br: 67 Photo/Alamy; 26tr: Library of Congress; 27cr: Hugo de Wolf/Shutterstock; 28c: iStockphoto; 28cl: Gerald Bloncourt/Rue des Archives; 29cr: BrazilPhotos.com/Alamy; 29tc: Tom Hahn/iStockphoto; 30bc: Jeremy Horner/Corbis; 31tl: Rober Byron/iStockphoto; 32bl: NASA; 32tl: Demid/Shutterstock; 33br: Alvey Towers Picture Library/Alamy; 33tl: Michael Maloney/San Fransico Chronicle/Corbis; 34cr: Goran Yankovich/Alamy; 34tl: Hulton-Deutsch Collection/Corbis; 34bl: Yue Yuewei/Xinhua Press/Coris; 34c: Betacam-SP/Shutterstock; 35c: The Photolibrary Wales/Alamy; 35tr: Patricia Hofmeester/Shutterstock; 35cr: Rhett Sutphin/Wikipedia; 36bl: Fredrik Renander/Alamy; 37bc: Loie Pisihoyos/Corbis; 38tr: America/Alamy; 38tc: iStockphoto; 38cl: TheSupe87/Shutterstock; 38bc: Laurence Grayson/Wikipedia; 39rc: GoGo Images Corporation/Alamy; 40bc: Robert Harding Picture Library Ltd/Alamy; 41tr: Chad Ehlers/Alamy; 41tl: Victorian Traditions/Shutterstock; 41c: Suravid/Shutterstock; 41bl: Nikola Bilic/Shutterstock; 41br: Sheldon Gardner/Shutterstock; 42bc: Photos 12/Alamy; 42tc: Orca/Shutterstock; 43tr: Bettmann/Corbis; 43cr: Salvatore Di Nolfi/epa/Corbis; 43bl: Rainer Plendl/Shutterstock; 43c: Larry D Moore/Wikipedia

The author would like to give very many thanks to Mary Platt for her research, support and perceptive advice.

He would like to thank Mitchel Kalmanson at the Lester Kalmanson Agency for his advice about the risks of working with circus animals.